ANIMALS ON THE BRINK
Blue Whales

Patricia Miller-Schroeder

www.av2books.com

AV² provides enriched content that supplements and complements this book. Weigl's AV² books strive to create inspired learning and engage young minds in a total learning experience.

Your AV² Media Enhanced books come alive with...

 Audio
Listen to sections of the book read aloud.

 Key Words
Study vocabulary, and complete a matching word activity.

 Video
Watch informative video clips.

 Quizzes
Test your knowledge.

 Embedded Weblinks
Gain additional information for research.

 Slide Show
View images and captions, and prepare a presentation.

 Try This!
Complete activities and hands-on experiments.

... and much, much more!

Go to **www.av2books.com,** and enter this book's unique code.

BOOK CODE

E627720

AV² by Weigl brings you media enhanced books that support active learning.

Published by AV² by Weigl
350 5th Avenue, 59th Floor
New York, NY 10118
Website: www.av2books.com   www.weigl.com

Library of Congress Control Number: 2012940073

ISBN 978-1-61913-423-2 (hard cover)
ISBN 978-1-61913-424-9 (soft cover)

Printed in the United States of America in North Mankato, Minnesota
1 2 3 4 5 6 7 8 9   16 15 14 13 12

052012
WEP170512

Project Coordinator Aaron Carr
Design Mandy Christiansen

Every reasonable effort has been made to trace ownership and to obtain permission to reprint copyright material. The publishers would be pleased to have any errors or omissions brought to their attention so that they may be corrected in subsequent printings.

Photo Credits
Weigl acknowledges Getty Images as its primary photo supplier for this title.

Contents

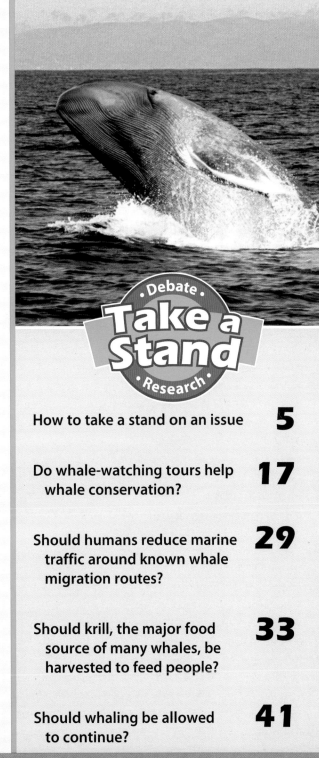

Take a Stand
Debate · Research

The Blue Whale

Whales have fascinated people for centuries. They were seen as mysterious creatures that lived under the waves far out at sea. Sailors told stories of their huge size and fierce nature. Many people thought whales were sea monsters. Today, people still have much to learn about whales. One of the least known of these ocean giants is the blue whale.

In this book you will learn about the largest animal in the world. You will learn how creatures as large as a jet plane feast on tiny animals no bigger than your finger. Follow blues thousands of miles to warm seas where 2-ton (1,814-kilogram) calves are born. Learn how they keep in touch with one another over hundreds of miles (kilometers) of ocean. Explore the many dangers that blue whales face in their changing natural environment. Read on to enter the watery world of the blue whale.

Blue whales are one of the great whales, a group of the largest whales in the world. Other great whales include right whales, gray whales, and humpback whales.

Most often, the only part of a blue whale people see is its spout, back, or fin.

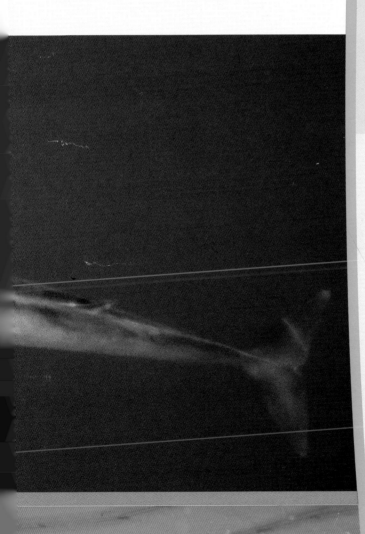

How to Take a Stand on an Issue

Research is important to the study of any scientific field. When scientists choose a subject to study, they must conduct research to ensure they have a thorough understanding of the topic. They ask questions about the subject and then search for answers. Sometimes, however, there is no clear answer to a question. In these cases, scientists must use the information they have to form a hypothesis, or theory. They must take a stand on one side of an issue or the other. Follow the process below for each Take a Stand section in this book to determine where you stand on these issues.

1. **What is the Issue?**
    a. Determine a research subject, and form a general question about the subject.

2. **Form a Hypothesis**
    a. Search at the library and online for sources of information on the subject.
    b. Conduct basic research on the subject to narrow down the general question.
    c. Form a hypothesis on the subject based on research to this point.
    d. Make predictions based on the hypothesis. What are the expected results?

3. **Research the Issue**
    a. Conduct extensive research using a variety of sources, including books, scientific journals, and reliable websites.
    b. Collect data on the issue and take notes on all information gathered from research.
    c. Draw conclusions based on the information collected.

4. **Conclusion**
    a. Explain the research findings.
    b. Was the hypothesis proved or disproved?

Tale of the Whale

Scientists believe whales came from the same group of prehistoric animals as deer and cows.

A blue whale swims by moving its powerful tail up and down in the water. When the whale dives from the surface, it sometimes raises its tail above water.

Features

Whales are a variety of sizes, from 6-foot (1.8-m) long dolphins to the largest whale ever recorded, a 100-foot (30.5-m) long blue whale. All whales are **streamlined** and well adapted for living in water.

Many people once thought whales were huge fish. People now know that whales are not fish. They are mammals, like dogs, horses, lions, and humans. Like all mammals, they are warm-blooded creatures that breathe air. They also give birth to live young that drink milk from their mothers' bodies. Being a mammal poses special problems for an animal that spends its entire life in water. The blue whale, like all other whales, has solved these problems with many special features.

Blue whales are the largest animals in the world. The largest blue whale ever recorded weighed more than 150 tons (136,000 kg). This is bigger than most dinosaurs. Only one dinosaur, the seismosaurus, may have been larger. However, most of the really big blues were killed by whalers. The average size of blue whales today is about 70 to 85 feet (21.3 to 25.9 m).

Blue whales can grow to this enormous size because they live in the ocean. The water helps support their large weight. A blue whale will die if it is stranded on land. Its bones cannot support its body and will collapse, crushing its internal organs. Blue whales are big on the inside as well. A blue's heart is the size of a sports car, and its arteries are as large as drainpipes. Its tongue weighs 4 tons (3,628 kg) and is strong enough to hold an adult elephant.

No one is sure how long blue whales live. Some experts estimate that they live 60 to 70 years, but their life span may be longer. Blue whales are sometimes attacked by killer whales. Some are injured by collisions with ships, and others get entangled in nets. A serious threat to blue whales comes from pollution and oil spills.

Classification

Blue whales have many relatives. There are about 78 **species** of whales and dolphins. They all belong to the order of animals called the **Cetacea**. The Cetacea is divided into two suborders. These are the toothed whales and the **baleen** whales. Baleen whales do not have teeth, although they are born with tiny tooth buds that never grow. Scientists believe this is evidence that toothed and baleen whales have evolved from a common toothed ancestor. Toothed whales catch and eat fish and squid. Baleen whales filter small creatures from the water with their huge mouths.

Blue whales are baleen whales. Blues are part of a group of baleen whales called **rorquals**. The rorquals are among the fastest whales in the oceans. They all have a pleated throat pouch that expands when they are feeding. Other rorquals are the fin, sei, Bryde's, humpback, and minke whales.

There is only one species of blue whale. Its Latin, or scientific name, is *Balaenoptera musculus*. Some scientists recognize a smaller subspecies called the pygmy blue whale, or *Balaenoptera musculus brevicauda*.

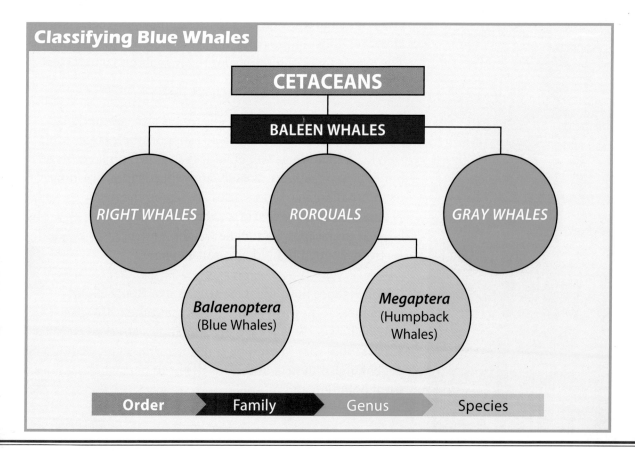

Classifying Blue Whales

CETACEANS

BALEEN WHALES

RIGHT WHALES   RORQUALS   GRAY WHALES

Balaenoptera (Blue Whales)   *Megaptera* (Humpback Whales)

Order   Family   Genus   Species

Cetaceans are named for the Greek word *ketos*, which means "sea monster." The scientific name for toothed whales means "sea monsters with teeth." The scientific name for baleen whales means "sea monsters with mustaches."

A blue whale's baleen grows throughout its life.

Powerful muscles open and close the blue whale's blowholes so that water does not get into the whale's lungs.

Special Adaptations

A whale spends its whole life in the ocean. It has more special adaptations for living in water than any other mammal. Almost every part of the blue whale's body has adapted to suit its underwater habitat.

Blubber

Just beneath their skin, blue whales have a thick layer of fat called blubber. Blubber helps to keep whales warm. This is important because animals lose heat 25 times faster in water than on land. Blue whales put on blubber when they feed in the **polar oceans**. This is a good way to store food during their long **migrations**, when they eat very little.

Flukes

The whale's powerful tail is made of two **flukes**. The tail is flat and rigid and lies horizontally. It moves up and down when the whale swims. This motion moves the whale through the water. The huge flukes of blue whales are usually 18 feet (5.5 m) across.

Streamlined Bodies

Despite their large size, blue whales are slim and streamlined. Their smooth, torpedo shape and powerful muscles let them glide easily through the water. One of the fastest of the great whales, blues can reach speeds of 30 miles (50 kilometers) per hour.

Blowholes

A whale breathes through nostrils on the top of its head. The blue whale, like all baleen whales, has two openings. Toothed whales have only one. These openings are called blowholes because they are used to blow out old, stale air from the whale's lungs. This air comes out in a fine, misty spray called a **spout**, or a blow. Blue whales' spouts can blow 30 feet (9.1 m) into the air.

Baleen

Like all baleen whales, blue whales do not have teeth. Instead, they eat with the help of a special substance called baleen. Baleen is made of strong **keratin**, which also makes up human fingernails and hair. It grows in long strips from the whale's upper jaw. The strips fit closely together and are lined with bristles. When the whale gulps water into its mouth, the baleen acts like a filter. The whale then closes its mouth, forcing the water out through the baleen strips. The bristles trap anything that is too large to fit through the filter. This is how blue whales trap the tiny **krill** they eat.

Tale of the Whale

Each whale species has a distinctive spout. An experienced whale watcher can tell what kind of whale is below the surface by its spout. The spout of a blue whale is a straight column, 30 feet (9.1 meters) tall.

Although observers can sometimes see several blue whales swimming close together, they cannot always tell whether the whales are related.

Groups

Most of what people know about whales has been learned from dead whales. A great deal is therefore known about their physical features. Much less is known about their social behavior. Scientists have started some long-term studies on whales living in the wild. These studies are giving a fascinating look into the lives of many species of whales. Most studies of whales have been on toothed whales such as dolphins, killer whales, and sperm whales. A few studies have now begun on some of the baleen whales.

Great whales live a long time, so studying their family life can take decades. The longest running study on blue whales is now taking place along the St. Lawrence River in Quebec, Canada. Scientists there have photographed more than 350 individual blues and are learning how to tell them apart. Other studies on blue whales are being done in the Sea of Cortez, Mexico, and off the California coast. So far, however, the social relationships and mating behavior of blue whales are mostly unknown.

Many of the toothed whales studied appear to be very social creatures. They live in groups or families called pods. The blue whale, however, seems to be quite solitary. Outside of the mother-calf bond, little has been learned about relationships among blues.

Observers have often noted two blues swimming quite close together. These pairs are normally within 50 to 100 feet (15.2 to 30.5 m) of each other, although the distance can vary greatly. Some pairs have been seen up to 1 mile (1.6 km) or more apart. The pairs may be related individuals, such as siblings, or two mates. A few may be mothers and calves. No one knows for sure. Sometimes, several blue whales will be found feeding on a large school of krill. These may be only temporary groups gathering at a good food source. Scientists have observed 15 to 30 blues in a 5- to 10-square-mile (13- to 26-square-kilometer) area.

Whales are so huge that it is likely each whale needs a large feeding area to itself. It is possible that, during the feeding season, the whales must spread out to get enough to eat. Once they migrate to their breeding area, it is possible that larger groups may form. They do not eat much during this time, so they could form larger groups. However, they may stay scattered on the breeding ground with only mates coming together.

Communication

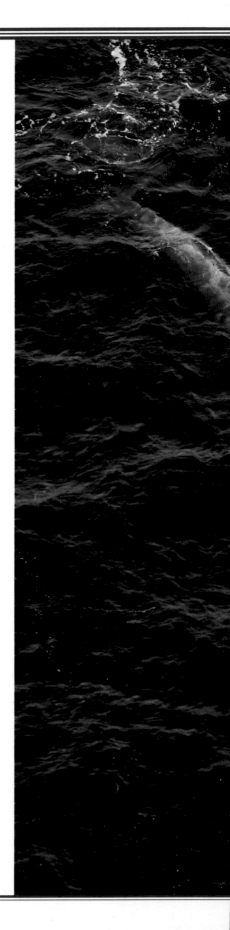

Some whales, like the humpback, communicate with long, complicated songs. Some toothed whales can hear and send ultrasonic sounds. These sounds are too high-pitched for humans to hear. Scientists think that blue whales also have many ways to communicate with one another across long distances. They make a variety of clicking and moaning calls. They also make noises by forcing air out of their blowholes or by slapping the water with their **flippers** or flukes.

Blue whales make low-pitched moans. These are deep and complex sounds. They may be the loudest and lowest in the animal kingdom. Blue whales can make sounds that are louder than a jet aircraft. The moans can last between 15 and 38 seconds. They are carried through the ocean for hundreds of miles (kilometers).

Low frequency sound travels well in the ocean. In water, the speed of sound is five times faster than in air. The returning echoes may tell the whales where islands, shorelines, or other animals are located. The sounds may also be heard and answered by other whales. This may be how whales that are far apart communicate with each other. Scientists are not sure what blue whales are communicating with their calls. Some think they may tell one another about the location of good food sources, such as a school of krill. Others think they warn of danger or keep a widely spaced group together.

Blue whales probably use sound to help them find food. Unlike dolphins, they do not use true **echolocation**. However, either the sounds the blues make or the sounds made by their food may guide them as they travel through the ocean.

Tale of the Whale

Scientists think male blue whales may use low-pitch calls to attract females for mating.

Except for mother and calf pairs, most blue whales live on their own. They use very low-pitched called to communicate with one another from up to 1,000 miles (1,600 km) away.

Body Language

Many whales share certain signals and behaviors that are likely important in communicating. These behaviors are learned and practiced in play by young whales. Blues have not been observed in some of these behaviors as often as other whales. Breaching is the most commonly observed behavior in blues, and even it is rare to see.

Lobtailing

Lobtailing is when a whale raises its tail fluke out of the water and splashes it down on the surface. This may have more than one purpose. Some toothed whales use lobtailing to herd fish. Other whales may do this to signal others or show aggression.

Spyhopping

Most whales stick their head above the surface of the water. This is called spyhopping. It lets them look above the water's surface. They may be checking to see where other whales are and what they are doing. Sometimes, they may just be curious about a boat or something else on the surface of the water.

Breaching

When a whale leaps out of the water and lands with a splash, it is called breaching. This is often done when other whales are nearby. Many young whales start breaching when they are only a few weeks old.

Flippering

This is a common activity and may be done with lobtailing. The whale lies on its side and raises a flipper above the water's surface. The flipper is then used to strike the water several times, causing noisy splashes.

Take a Stand
Debate • Research

Do whale-watching tours help whale conservation?

Whale-watching tours take groups of people out into the ocean to see whales closeup. People taking the tours hope to see whales breaching, spyhopping, flippering, and lobtailing. However, some people complain that whale watchers harass the whales. They think that the tours should be stopped or kept from coming too near the whales.

FOR

1. People who see whales up close come away with a new respect and appreciation for whales. These people will want to help save whales from extinction.
2. Whale-watching provides income for people and communities. It shows those who used to depend on whaling that whales are worth more alive than dead.

AGAINST

1. People can appreciate whales from a distance. When people get too close, they may disturb the whales or even draw the attention of predators, such as killer whales, to the blue whales.
2. The more thrilling the experience, the more money the tour operator makes. Some operators may be tempted to approach whales too closely and take risks in order to increase their profits.

Tale of the Whale

A blue whale calf is as big as a full-grown elephant. When a blue whale is full grown, it is as big as 30 elephants.

During its first year of life, a blue whale calf must stay with its mother for food and protection.

Mating and Birth

Blue whales mate during their winter breeding season. This is likely to be November to February for whales that live in the northern hemisphere and May to August for whales that live in the southern hemisphere. Biologists do not know if a blue whale female mates with just one male or many. Blue whales have been seen traveling in pairs. Sometimes, however, partners in the pair change. For this reason, scientists do not know if blue whales are **monogamous**. Whale experts now believe blue whales may be monogamous for short periods of time.

Both females and males are ready to mate when they are about 10 years old. Females give birth to one calf every two or three years.

The **gestation** time for blue whales is 11 or 12 months. Pregnant whales leave their polar-feeding grounds and travel to warmer waters to give birth. When the mothers reach the calving grounds, a single calf is born. Blue whale calves are the largest infants in the animal kingdom.

Giving birth to an air-breathing infant in the ocean causes special problems. Calves are born tailfirst and are pushed to the surface by their mothers. This helps the infants to take their first breaths. Calves can swim right after birth.

From an Expert

"When you are in the water and see a blue whale pass very close, it's a bit like standing on a train platform watching the train go by, hoping that the wind isn't going to suck you under its wheels." - Roger Payne

Roger Payne is one of the world's leading experts on whales. He is president of the Whale Conservation Institute and is a scientific adviser to the International Whaling Commission. He has led more than 100 ocean expeditions and has studied all species of large whales. He has written many scientific articles on whales as well as a book called *Among Whales*.

Calves

Many land mammals are born helpless. They may be safely hidden in nests or carried by their mothers to protect them from harm. Whale infants, however, must be active and alert from birth. They need to be able to swim and follow their mothers. They have much to learn, and they must learn it quickly.

The blue whale calf and mother spend most of their time alone. They may occasionally be joined by other whales. Scientists do not know how adult blues treat calves on the calving grounds. They do know that the bond between mother and infant is strong. Like most mammal infants, a whale infant depends on its mother for food and protection.

A newborn blue whale is as big as many full-grown whales of other species. Despite its size, it depends on its mother for food and protection. Its baleen plates have not grown yet, so it cannot feed itself. For the next eight months, the calf lives on its mother's milk. During this time, it stays close to its mother.

The mother produces milk in nipples that are hidden in a slit on her abdomen. The calf nurses every few hours by pushing its mouth against the slit. The mother's milk is very rich in fat and vitamins. The young whale grows quickly while it nurses.

For at least six to eight months, the young whale depends on its mother to protect it from killer whales and large sharks. During this time, the calf learns how to feed, avoid predators, and communicate with other whales. It also begins to learn the long migration routes it will travel every year.

During its first year of life, a blue whale calf can gain about 200 pounds (91 kilograms) each day.

Tale of the **Whale**

Blue whale calves may seem to grow right before your eyes. Calves gain 8 pounds (3.6 kg) an hour while they are nursing.

Blue whale calves can weigh up to 3 tons (2.7 tonnes) and stretch to 25 feet (8 meters) long.

Development

Birth – 8 Months

At birth, a newborn blue whale is about 20 to 25 feet (6.1 to 7.6 m) long, and weighs about 5,500 pounds (2,495 kg). The calf drinks 50 gallons (189 l) of its mother's rich milk each day. While nursing, it gains 200 pounds (91 kg) a day, or about 8 pounds (3.6 kg) an hour. The infant's skin is the same blue-gray as an adult's skin. Each calf has a distinctive spotted pattern on its flanks that it will carry throughout its life. By taking pictures of these patterns, scientists have learned to identify many individual blue whales. A calf's skin may be wrinkled at first, but it quickly becomes smooth and sleek. Its dorsal fin may be rubbery and bent over, but it soon straightens out. The calf swims well and follows its mother everywhere. It playfully practices adult behaviors like breaching and lobtailing.

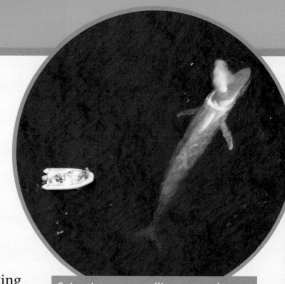

Scientists use satellites to track blue whale movements at various stages of their life cycle. To do this, scientists must get close enough to the whale to attach a tracking tag.

8 Months – 1 Year

By the time a calf is eight months old, it weighs 50,000 pounds (22,680 kg) and is about 50 feet (15.2 m) long. Its baleen plates have grown, and it is fully **weaned** and eating krill. The calf has migrated long distances with its mother to and from the feeding grounds. After eight months, most calves are quite independent.

1 Year – 10 Years

By the end of its first year, a young blue whale is on its own, although it sometimes may travel within 1 mile (1.6 km) or so of its mother. It is still growing and gaining weight as it becomes an adolescent. During feeding season, the young whale puts on about 88 pounds (40 kg) each day.

10+ Years

The whale is now an adult and is ready to breed. By this time, most females are about 79 feet (24 m) long, and most males are about 74 feet (22.4 m) long. Some of these young adults continue to grow. Few grow larger than 92 feet (28 m) long.

Birth – 8 Months

8 Months – 1 Year

10+ Years

Habitat

Blue whales travel widely and are found in a number of ocean environments. Part of their time is spent in the deep ocean. They can also be found in water close to shore and along continental shelves and ice fronts. Blues spend part of each year in cold Arctic or Antarctic water. They also spend part of the year in warm water near the **equator**.

Blue whales feed near the surface of the water. They are usually found within 300 feet (91 m) of the surface. Very rarely, they will dive much deeper, up to 3,000 feet (914 m). This behavior has been noted in blue whales that are frightened or in pain, such as when they have been harpooned.

Organizing the Ocean

Earth is home to millions of different organisms, all of which have specific survival needs. These organisms rely on their environment, or the place where they live, for their survival. All plants and animals have relationships with their environment. They interact with the environment itself, as well as the other plants and animals within the environment. These interactions create ecosystems.

Ecosystems can be broken down into levels of organization. These levels range from a single plant or animal to many species of plants and animals living together in an area.

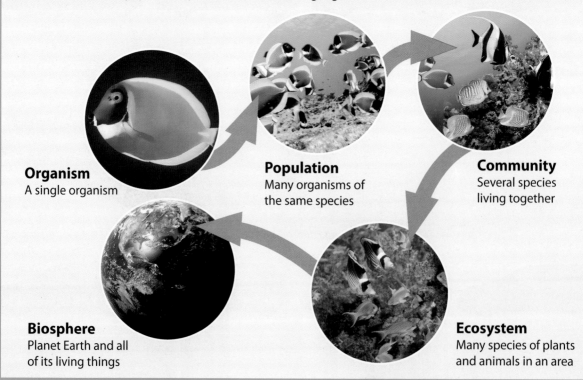

Organism
A single organism

Population
Many organisms of the same species

Community
Several species living together

Biosphere
Planet Earth and all of its living things

Ecosystem
Many species of plants and animals in an area

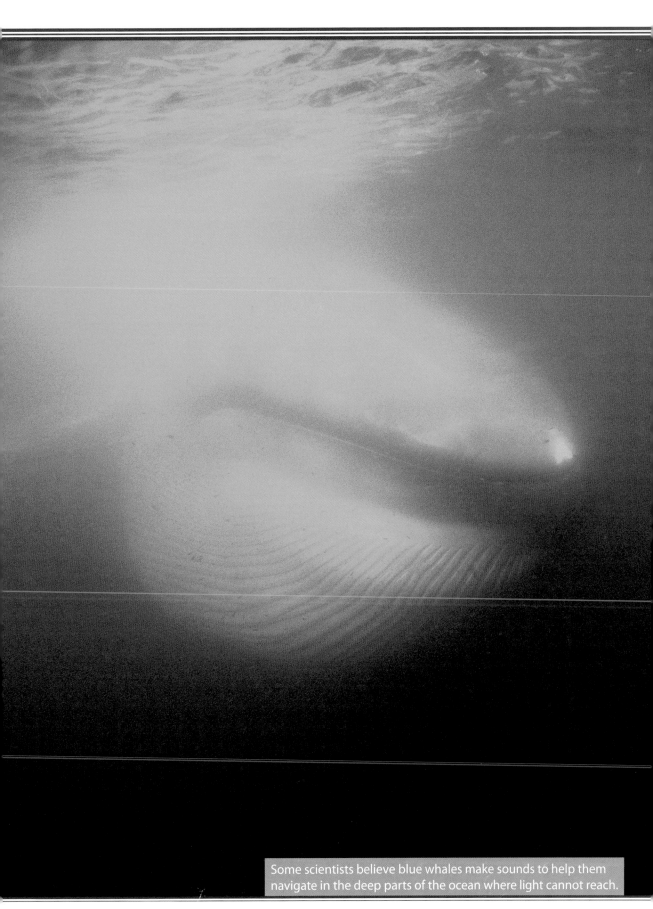

Some scientists believe blue whales make sounds to help them navigate in the deep parts of the ocean where light cannot reach.

Blue whales have one of the longest migration journeys of any mammal. This journey takes them from the polar regions to the equator.

Blue whales cover a vast range of ocean and can travel at speeds up to 30 miles (50 km) per hour. This makes it very challenging to spot blue whales in nature.

Range

Blue whales wander freely over great distances in the oceans. They do not appear to defend a home range or territory. When several blues are in the same area, such as near a good feeding source, they space themselves out.

There are three main populations of blue whales. These are the North Pacific, the North Atlantic, and the Antarctic populations. The North Pacific and Atlantic populations are each probably split into eastern and western groups. The Antarctic blues can probably be split into groups that range on either side of South America, Africa, and Australia.

The rich feeding grounds of the Antarctic Ocean used to be where most blue whales gathered. Today, perhaps only a few hundred blues survive in the whole Southern Ocean. There are still a few places where blue whales can be seen regularly every year. The best sites are in the St. Lawrence River in Quebec, Canada, and off the coasts of California and Mexico.

"Because of the nomadic nature of their existence, blue whales will, for a long time to come, reserve many surprises for those who study them. The parameters of their lives will be difficult to define, and this may be what appeals to those of us who study them." - Richard Sears

Richard Sears has been studying blue whales since the 1970s. He directs studies of blue whales at the Mingan Island Cetacean Study on the St. Lawrence River in Quebec, Canada, and in the Sea of Cortez, Mexico. He was the first to discover how to identify individual blue whales.

Migration

The blue whale's year is divided between two main seasons—the summer feeding season and the winter breeding and calving season. These two seasons are joined by long migrations. Whales that migrate to the northern hemisphere and whales that migrate to the south probably never meet. They are kept apart by continents and seasons. In April, the southern blue whales leave the Antarctic for warmer waters near the equator. They stay there until September, breeding and giving birth to their calves. At the same time that southern whales begin their journey north, northern whales leave the warm calving grounds. They head north for their feeding grounds in colder waters. Colder waters have more oxygen, which encourages animals such as plankton to grow. From October to March, the groups reverse their paths.

Blue Whale Migration Paths

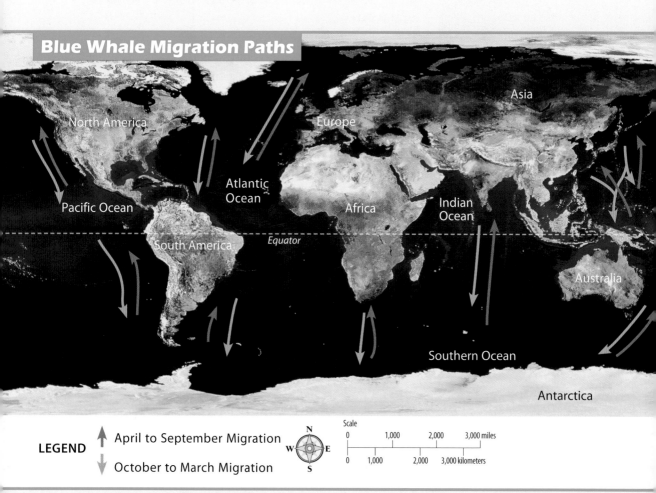

LEGEND

⬆ April to September Migration

⬇ October to March Migration

Scale

0   1,000   2,000   3,000 miles

0   1,000   2,000   3,000 kilometers

How Do Whales Migrate?

When whales migrate, they must find their way across thousands of miles (kilometers) of open ocean. The same whales often return to the same place each year. How do they navigate and find their way? One theory is that they somehow use Earth's magnetic fields as a guide. Earth has regular patterns of magnetic forces that whales may have some way of receiving. They may use these patterns to navigate through the oceans. How they do this is another whale mystery people have yet to solve.

Why Do Blue Whales Migrate?

Why do whales travel these great distances twice each year? Why do they leave rich feeding grounds and travel huge distances to places where there is less food?

Many scientists think the icy waters of the feeding grounds are too cold and stormy for calves. Others believe that, thousands of years ago, the whales' feeding and calving grounds were closer together. Over time, changes in the ocean's temperature caused less food to be available in the warmer oceans. At the same time, more food became available in the colder oceans. The whales sought more abundant food sources in these areas. However, when it was time to mate or give birth, they traveled back to their familiar calving areas. Perhaps both theories are true. Scientists have seen blues feeding with young calves in the Sea of Cortez, a warm-water sea, so this migratory behavior may not apply to all whale populations.

Take a Stand
· Debate ·
· Research ·

Should humans reduce marine traffic around known whale migration routes?

Military ships use powerful pulses of sound called SONAR to navigate, and many transport ships have large engines. In recent years, scientists have discovered that these disruptions to the environment, called noise pollution, are harmful to whales. This issue is especially important because sound travels much farther underwater than it does in air.

FOR

1. SONAR helps submarines and military ships find their way, but it can also cause whales to become disoriented, or bleed internally. SONAR is thought to be one reason that whales beach themselves.
2. Loud noises from ship engines can cause whales to lose their way while migrating. There is some evidence that constant noise causes physical stress in whales, and makes it more difficult for them to breed.

AGAINST

1. Military SONAR is important to coastal defence. The United States Navy and Coast Guard use sonar to detect threats and keep people safe.
2. Many products consumed by people around the world arrive at their destinations in cargo ships. If there were restrictions placed on ship traffic, the global economy could suffer.

Diet

Everything about the blue whale is big, including its appetite. To maintain such a huge body, an adult blue whale needs to eat about 4 tons (3,628 kg) of krill each day during feeding season. At this time, whales gain extra blubber. They may increase their weight by 40 percent.

Krill measure only 1 to 2 inches (2.5 to 5 cm) in length.

However, when blue whales leave the feeding grounds, many do not eat much for several months. Blues will feed if krill is available on the calving grounds, but there is normally little food in the warm oceans. Many blues will go for long periods of time without eating regularly. Whales can do this and survive because the water supports their large weight. This means that they use very little energy to swim. In addition, whales are insulated by thick blubber. This means they do not use much energy to keep warm. Scientists now believe that some whales may stay in krill-rich waters year-round.

How do blue whales eat such huge meals of krill? They have the help of the largest mouth in the animal kingdom. The jaws of an 80-foot (24.4-m) whale can be 22 to 24 feet (6.7 to 7.3 m) long. The blue whale has a muscular throat pouch that has folds of skin that look like pleats. The loose skin inside the pleats allows the throat to expand like a balloon while the whale is feeding. All rorqual whales have a pleated throat pouch.

When a blue whale finds a school of krill or other food, it opens its huge mouth wide. Its throat expands, and the whale gulps in water and krill. A blue may take in as much as 66 tons (59,862 kg) of water and food in one gulp. The whale then closes its mouth and contracts its throat pleats, forcing out the water through its baleen plates. The whale uses its tongue to help squeeze the water out. Anything too large to pass among the baleen plates is trapped. The whale then swallows the huge load of krill and other food trapped in its mouth. Each giant mouthful provides the whale with hundreds of pounds (kilograms) of krill.

Tale of the Whale

Blue whales have more blubber than many other types of whales. The most oil ever made from the blubber of one blue whale was 50 tons (45,350 kg).

A blue whale can eat as many as four million krill in one day.

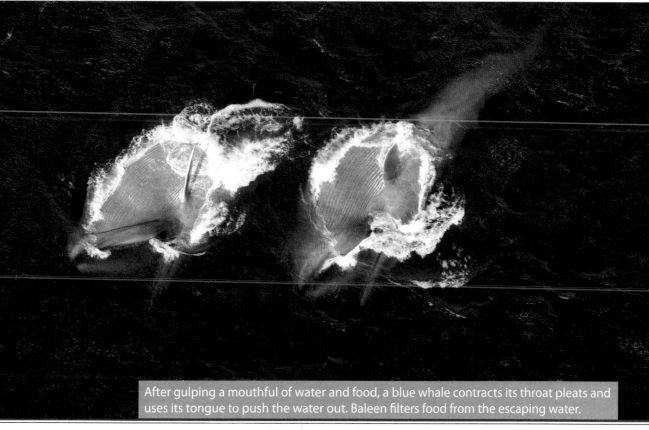

After gulping a mouthful of water and food, a blue whale contracts its throat pleats and uses its tongue to push the water out. Baleen filters food from the escaping water.

The Food Cycle

A food cycle shows how energy in the form of food is passed from one living thing to another. Blue whales are carnivores, although the animals they eat are tiny. As they feed and move through the oceans, blue whales affect the lives of other living things. In the diagram below, the blue arrows show the flow of energy from one living thing to the next through a **food web**.

Parasites
Blue whales provide a home for "hitchhikers," such as barnacles and whale lice.

Secondary Consumers
Blue whales eat krill and provide food for other living things.

Decomposers
When a whale dies, its body sinks to the ocean floor to add to the nutrients that cause plankton to thrive.

Producers
Tiny plants and animals called plankton live in the ocean. They eat nutrients from the ocean floor in polar areas.

Take a Stand

Debate • Research

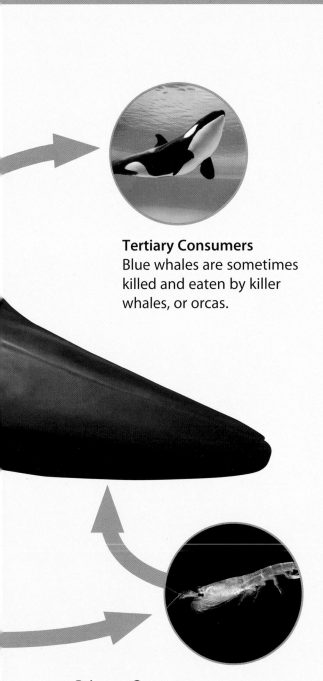

Tertiary Consumers
Blue whales are sometimes killed and eaten by killer whales, or orcas.

Primary Consumers
Small, shrimplike krill eat smaller plankton and are then eaten by blue and other whales.

Should krill, the major food source of many whales, be harvested to feed people?

Krill is a major food source for many marine animals. It is also the main food source for blue whales. Earth's human population is five billion people and still growing. Many people do not have enough to eat. Some experts suggest a major krill harvest as a way to feed many of the world's hungry. However, a commercial krill fishery would remove huge numbers of krill from the ocean. These krill would be removed from the food chains of the animals that depend on them, including blue whales.

FOR

1. Many of the world's poor cannot move to obtain more food. Animals such as blue whales are free to follow other food sources.
2. The number of whales living in the oceans has been greatly reduced by whaling. This reduced population does not need as many krill.

AGAINST

1. Animals have adapted over long periods of time to eating certain foods. They often cannot switch to another food source or change where they live or migrate.
2. Blue whales were almost destroyed by whaling. Their populations will not recover if their major food source is also destroyed.

Tale of the Whale

Most information on whale sizes came from whales killed by whalers. Weights were estimated by weighing chopped-off chunks of meat and adding a few tons (tonnes) for lost blood.

As the largest animal ever to have lived on Earth, blue whales have little to fear from most of the other animals that live in the ocean. Killer whales hunting in a pack are one of the few natural dangers blue whales face.

Competition

Blue whales may seem to have unlimited food and living space in the oceans. However, blues sometimes compete actively with other blues for food and mates. Blue whales have little to fear from most marine animals. They are too large and too fast for almost all ocean predators. Only killer whales hunting in packs and human whalers have been able to kill blue whales. Today, it is humans' careless use of the oceans that is most threatening to the blue whale's habitat and food supply.

Researchers believe that blue whales must sometimes compete with one another for food and mates. However, such competition is difficult to measure and may be too subtle for human observers. There are fewer than 8,000 blue whales living in the world's oceans, so competition may be unnecessary most of the time.

Blues share their feeding grounds with other whale species, such as minke, fin, and humpback whales. Blues sometimes compete with these other whales, especially fins, for food. The fins' main diet is krill and other tiny, hard-shelled animals called crustaceans. However, most baleen whales feed on a wider variety of food than the blue whales, so they have more choice of things to eat. Blue whales avoid killer whales, which are their main ocean predators.

From an Expert

Erich Hoyt is one of Canada's top nature writers. He has written many articles on whales and several books, including *Meeting the Whales*. He is also a member of the Society for Marine Mammalogy.

"Often another blue is seen a kilometer or more away from a lone blue. Maybe blues, the largest animals on Earth, simply live life on a much bigger scale. Their low blasts carry easily for kilometers underwater. Perhaps they are all in close touch, or as close as they need to be..." - Erich Hoyt

Blue Whales with Other Animals

The blue whale comes in contact with many other animals as it travels in the ocean. Many species of fish, dolphins, seals, and seabirds share the blue whale's home. The blue mainly sticks to its routine of feeding or raising calves. It leaves the other animals to go about their business in peace.

The blue whale itself provides a home for small creatures such as barnacles and whale lice. Barnacles attach themselves to the whale's skin. They travel with it and draw in food from the water. Whale lice look like tiny crabs. They dig into the whale's skin, feeding on it. The whale lice and barnacles do not really harm the whale, although they are likely irritating. Some humpback whales have been observed with raw chins after rubbing off barnacles. The blue is a fast-moving whale, so it does not have as many of these hitchhikers as slower whales, such as the gray and the humpback. Blues also sometimes give a little fish called a remora, or whalesucker, a ride. The remora attaches itself to the whale's side and harmlessly travels with it.

The remora uses a suction disk on its head to attach to whales, sharks, and even boats.

Tale of the **Whale**

For whales, breathing is not automatic, like it is for humans or other mammals. Whales must think to breathe.

The blue whale's spout is taller and thinner than the spout of most other whales. It is also very loud.

Folklore

Since ancient times, whales have been seen as mysterious creatures. Small whales, such as dolphins, often came close to shore. They were thought to be strange but friendly creatures. The large whales, however, were seen as dangerous sea monsters. They were only known from sailors' scary stories or when a dead whale was found onshore. A dead whale was often thought to be a bad omen. In many cultures, large whales represented something to be feared and conquered.

Whales have appeared in stories for more than 2,000 years. Aristotle, a Greek philosopher, recognized that whales were mammals 2,400 years ago. However, many ancient people believed whales were giant fish or sea monsters. Whales were often portrayed in pictures with huge, dragonlike mouths and tails. Stories were told of how whales would lure fish to their mouths with their sweet breath. Other stories were told of sailors mistaking whales for islands. When the sailors landed and made a fire, the whale would dive under the water, taking the sailors with it. Based on these tales, whales were thought to be animals that could not be trusted. They were seen as powerful enemies to be overcome. Killing a whale was considered heroic. It was not until the last few decades that people began to learn what whales are really like.

Early knowledge of whales came from sailors' stories of fierce sea monsters.

Myth	VS	Fact

Whales are fierce creatures that will attack and destroy boats and people.

Whales are generally peaceful creatures that seem to be friendly to humans. They often seek contact with whale watchers or people in small boats. However, whales that have been harpooned or those whose young are threatened can be dangerous.

Whales such as the blue could swallow people because of their huge size and gigantic mouths.

The blue whale and other baleen whales are able to expand their huge throat pouches and take in tons (tonnes) of water at a time. However, their throat opening is very small. Whales would be unable to swallow something as large as a person. They would not be able to chew up a person either, because they have no teeth.

Whales must come up to the surface to breathe, so they do not sleep.

Whales do sleep, although how they breathe while sleeping is still unknown. One theory is that sleeping whales float near the surface of the water, taking catnaps between breaths. Another theory is that they may rest only one-half of their brain at a time while sleeping. The half that is not resting prompts them to breathe.

In Herman Melville's novel *Moby Dick*, Captain Ahab searches the world for the sperm whale that caused him to lose his leg. Captain Ahab becomes obsessed with killing Moby Dick, and he dies in a dramatic fight with the giant whale. *Moby Dick* has become one of the best-known whale stories in modern times.

In 1994, the International Whaling Commission declared most of the southern oceans a **sanctuary** for whales. The Southern Ocean Whale Sanctuary now protects whales in one of their most important feeding areas. Sperm whales and almost all baleen whales that live in the southern hemisphere migrate to these oceans to feed every summer.

The great whales were once abundant in every ocean of the world. Before modern whaling began, there were about 250,000 to 300,000 blue whales. Today, blue whales are **endangered**. Scientists estimate that there are only 4,000 to 8,000 blues left in the world. The greatest loss occurred in the southern oceans, where the population was once 200,000. There, whales fed on rich stores of Antarctic krill.

Whale Sanctuary

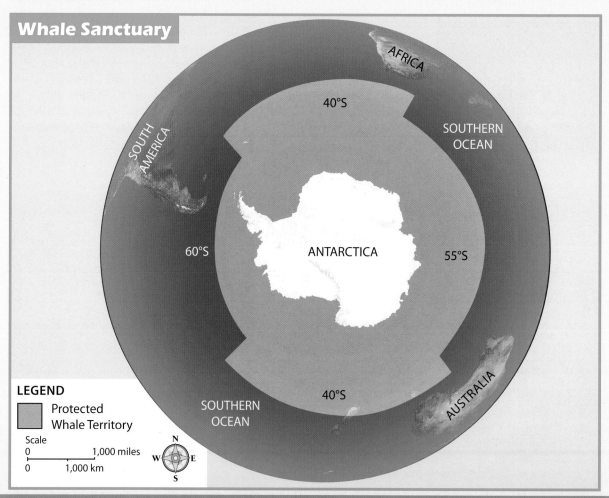

LEGEND

Protected Whale Territory

Scale
0 ——————— 1,000 miles
0 ——————— 1,000 km

The whalers followed blues there, killing huge numbers of whales. Today, fewer than 1,000 blue whales remain in the southern oceans. Their numbers have not grown much in the 30 years that blue whales have been protected.

Whales have been hunted by humans for more than 2,000 years. Whale blubber was prized because it could be made into oil that was used to make soap, candles, and lipstick. Whales were also killed for their baleen. Baleen was used to make many items, such as brushes and umbrella ribs. Baleen was once used for many things that are now made from plastic. Whale meat was used as pet food. Many people liked to eat it as well.

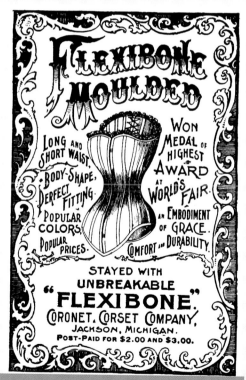

The baleen from whales has been used to make many items, including ladies' corsets.

Take a Stand

Debate · *Research*

Should whaling be allowed to continue?

Blue whales are still endangered, but other species of whales have larger and more stable populations. Scientists estimate that there are several hundred thousand minke whales living today, for example. Some people believe that humans should still be allowed to hunt these less-threatened whales.

FOR

1. Some remote or aboriginal communities depend on traditional methods of gathering food to sustain themselves. In some cases, these methods involve hunting whales.
2. A single whale can provide a large number of resources. When done on a small scale, commercial whaling can be an important source of income for coastal communities.

AGAINST

1. Whales must eat large amounts of food to sustain themselves. If too many whales are removed from an ecosystem, the animals they eat will reproduce unchecked, unbalancing the food webs. This can cause other animals to die out and may destroy entire fisheries.
2. Whales are large animals with strong bodies. Even with modern technology, it is difficult for whalers to kill a whale humanely. Opponents argue that whaling causes unneeded suffering.

Saving the Blue Whale

Today, blue whales cannot legally be hunted. Whaling is no longer a threat to the blue whale's survival, although some whales may have been illegally hunted since 1966. Now, there are new dangers. Human pollution of the oceans is the largest threat to blue whales. Toxic chemicals often end up in the ocean, where they poison the whales' food supply. When whales eat, the poison becomes concentrated in their bodies. Mother whales pass poisons to their calves through their milk. Whales may also swallow garbage floating in the ocean near their feeding areas.

Offshore oil drilling, oil spills, and toxic chemicals are deadly threats to whales and other ocean animals.

Oil spills can pollute large stretches of ocean. The oil can cling to the whales' skin, making them sick. It also poisons their food and destroys their habitat. Many ocean animals die in oil spills.

The use of drift nets is another problem. Drift nets are up to 30 miles (50 km) long. Fishers drag these huge nets in the ocean, creating a death trap for many marine mammals. Drift nets are especially dangerous for calves, but even large whales can become trapped and drown. A young female blue whale was found dead after getting tangled in a fishnet in the St. Lawrence River in 1991.

Whales became a symbol for the conservation movement in the 1970s. In 1971, a conservation group called the Animal Welfare Institute launched a worldwide Save the Whale campaign. This campaign encouraged people to boycott companies that used sperm whale oil to make products. Another group called Greenpeace tried to stop whale hunts. Greenpeace activists would zoom in between hunters and whales in rubber life rafts. Public pressure forced many companies to find other products to replace whale oil. Oil made from the jojoba plant, a desert shrub, is now used as a replacement for whale oil.

Despite efforts to save whales, it may be too late for some species. Blue whales take so long to grow and reproduce that their populations may never recover from the whale hunts. Today's problems of pollution only further threaten the recovery of whale populations. A few populations may be increasing slightly, but their numbers remain very small. Scientists still have not seen a recovery of the blue whale population, even though legal hunting ended more than 30 years ago. In places where the populations were greatly reduced, the blues may have a hard time even finding mates.

Tale of the Whale

Baleen was sometimes called whalebone. It was often used to make corsets. Corsets are rigid undergarments once worn by many women to make themselves look slim.

Many animal rights organizations around the world hold rallies in an attempt to end whaling.

Back From the Brink

The first long-term study of the blue whale is being done in the Gulf of St. Lawrence, in Canada. The study is part of the Mingan Island Cetacean Study headed by Richard Sears. Sears and his research team have photographed and identified more than 350 blue whales since 1979. They have learned that many of the same whales return to the St. Lawrence every year to feed. The research team is also studying blue whales in the Sea of Cortez, in Mexico. They have identified more than 325 blues in that area.

You can help them learn about blue whales and even become a part of the research team by adopting one of the blue whales in their study. Whales may be adopted by school classes or by individuals. As a foster parent to a blue whale, you receive a photo and information about your whale. You also receive a newsletter about the work of the whale researchers. Most of all, you get to help blue whales through the research program.

For more information on the blue whale research program or the "Adopt-a-Giant" program, contact:

Mingan Island Cetacean Study
285 Green Street
St. Lambert, Quebec
J4P 1T3
Canada

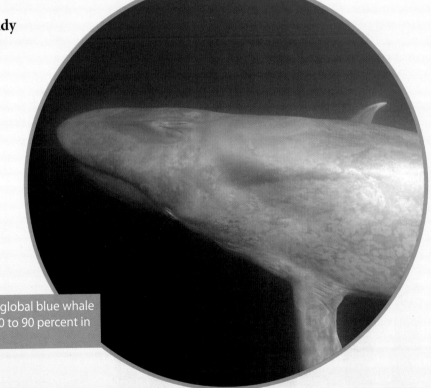

Scientists estimate that the global blue whale population has shrunk by 70 to 90 percent in the last century.

Activity

Debating helps people think about ideas thoughtfully and carefully. When people debate, two sides take a different viewpoint on a subject. Each side takes turns presenting arguments to support its view.

Use the Take a Stand sections found throughout this book as a starting point for debate topics. Organize your friends or classmates into two teams. One team will argue in favor of the topic, and the other will argue against. Each team should research the issue thoroughly using reliable sources of information, including books, scientific journals, and trustworthy websites. Take notes of important facts that support your side of the debate. Prepare your argument using these facts to support your opinion.

During the debate, the members of each team are given a set amount of time to make their arguments. The team arguing the For side goes first. They have five minutes to present their case. All members of the team should participate equally. Then, the team arguing the Against side presents its arguments. Each team should take notes of the main points the other team argues.

After both teams have made their arguments, they get three minutes to prepare their rebuttals. Teams review their notes from the previous round. The teams focus on trying to disprove each of the main points made by the other team using solid facts. Each team gets three minutes to make its rebuttal. The team arguing the Against side goes first. Students and teachers watching the debate serve as judges. They should try to judge the debate fairly using a standard score sheet, such as the example below.

Criteria	Rate: 1-10	Sample Comments
1. Were the arguments well organized?	8	logical arguments, easy to follow
2. Did team members participate equally?	9	divided time evenly between members
3. Did team members speak loudly and clearly?	3	some members were difficult to hear
4. Were rebuttals specific to the other team's arguments?	6	rebuttals were specific, more facts needed
5. Was respect shown for the other team?	10	all members showed respect to the other team

Quiz

1. Blue whales are part of what group of large whales?

2. Why are blue whales able to grow so large?

3. What do blue whales have instead of teeth?

4. What is the name of the fanned end of a blue whale's tail?

5. What is it called when a whale raises its flipper out of the water?

6. What is a blue whale's primary food?

7. What is one of the only dangers blue whales face from other animals in the ocean?

8. How long does a newborn blue whale stay with its mother?

9. What are the two main seasons of a blue whale's year?

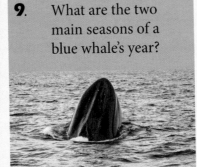

10. How many blue whales are believed to be alive today?

Answers:

1. Great whales 2. Water helps support their weight 3. Baleen 4. A fluke 5. Flippering 6. Krill 7. Killer whales, or orcas, hunting in a pack 8. About 1 year 9. The winter feeding season and the summer breeding season 10. Between 4,000 and 8,000

Key Words

baleen: a plate of keratin, frayed on one edge, in the mouth of a baleen whale

Cetacea: the large order of animals that includes all types of whales and dolphins

echolocation: the use of reflected sound waves to locate food and other objects

endangered: in danger of no longer existing anywhere on Earth

equator: an imaginary line around the center of Earth, dividing the northern and southern hemispheres

flippers: paddlelike forelimbs that help a whale steer through water

flukes: the flat, rigid part of a whale's tail; made up of two flukes

food web: connecting food chains; shows how energy flows from one organism to another through diet

gestation: the time it takes for an animal to develop inside its mother's womb

keratin: constantly growing substance that forms human nails and hair as well as the baleen of whales

krill: tiny, shrimplike animals that are the main food of many whales

migrations: moving regularly from one area to another

monogamous: having only one mate

polar oceans: cold oceans located near the North and South Poles

rorquals: a group of baleen whales with pleated throats that expand while feeding

sanctuary: a place of safety

species: groups of individuals with common characteristics

spout: misty spray blown into the air when a whale comes to the surface to breathe

streamlined: a simplified design to reduce resistance while moving through water

weaned: when a calf no longer nurses on its mother's milk

Index

Log on to www.av2books.com

AV² by Weigl brings you media enhanced books that support active learning. Go to www.av2books.com, and enter the special code found on page 2 of this book. You will gain access to enriched and enhanced content that supplements and complements this book. Content includes video, audio, weblinks, quizzes, a slide show, and activities.

Audio
Listen to sections of
the book read aloud.

Video
Watch informative video clips.

Embedded Weblinks
Gain additional information
for research.

Try This!
Complete activities and
hands-on experiments.

WHAT'S ONLINE?

Try This!	Embedded Weblinks	Video	EXTRA FEATURES
Chart the levels of organization within the biosphere.	Learn more about blue whales.	Watch a video about blue whales.	**Audio** Listen to sections of the book read aloud.
Map blue whale habitats around the world.	Read about blue whale conservation efforts.	See a blue whale in its natural habitat.	
Complete a food web for blue whales.	Find out more about blue whale habitats.		**Key Words** Study vocabulary, and complete a matching word activity.
Label and describe the parts of the blue whale.	Discover more fascinating facts about blue whales.		
Classify blue whales using a classification diagram.	Learn more about what you can do to help save blue whales.		**Slide Show** View images and captions, and prepare a presentation
			Quizzes Test your knowledge.

AV² was built to bridge the gap between print and digital. We encourage you to tell us what you like and what you want to see in the future.

Sign up to be an AV² Ambassador at www.av2books.com/ambassador.